Bible reflections
for older people

The Bible Reading Fellowship
15 The Chambers, Vineyard
Abingdon OX14 3FE
brf.org.uk

The Bible Reading Fellowship (BRF) is a Registered Charity (233280)

ISBN 978 1 80039 004 1

Acknowledgements
Scripture quotations marked with the following abbreviations are taken from the version shown. Where no abbreviation is given, the quotation is taken from the same version as the headline reference. **NIV**: The Holy Bible, New International Version (Anglicised edition) copyright © 1979, 1984, 2011 by Biblica. Used by permission of Hodder & Stoughton Publishers, a Hachette UK company. All rights reserved. 'NIV' is a registered trademark of Biblica. UK trademark number 1448790. **NRSV**: The New Revised Standard Version of the Bible, Anglicised edition, copyright © 1989, 1995 by the Division of Christian Education of the National Council of the Churches of Christ in the United States of America. Used by permission. All rights reserved.

Every effort has been made to trace and contact copyright owners for material used in this resource. We apologise for any inadvertent omissions or errors, and would ask those concerned to contact us so that full acknowledgement can be made in the future.

A catalogue record for this book is available from the British Library

Printed and bound in the UK by Zenith Media NP4 0DQ

Contents

About the writers

Ro Willoughby has been writing and editing Christian resources for many years. She has recently been licensed as a lay minister at St Chad's Woodseats in Sheffield, where she is engaged in ministry with people of all ages. It is a great joy that she now lives close to her children and grandchildren, as well as close to Bakewell and Chatsworth House, although she hasn't yet received an invitation to the ball!

John Rackley is associate minister to Christchurch LEP in Leicester. He acts as a supervisor for spiritual directors. He enjoys reading Rowan Williams and Philippa Gregory, Taizé-style worship, walking his dog Dougal and learning that life is fascinating from his grandchildren. BRF published his book *Seeking Faith, Finding God* in 2007, and he has written for *Guidelines*.

Margot Hodson is a vicar in the Oxford Diocese and is theology and education director for the John Ray Initiative (JRI), an educational organisation connecting environment, science and Christianity. **Martin Hodson** is a plant scientist and environmental biologist and has over 100 publications mostly in international science journals. He is operations director for JRI.
The Hodsons have published widely together on Christianity and the environment, including *A Christian Guide to Environmental Issues* (BRF, 2015; new edition 2021).

From the Editor

Welcome to this new collection of Bible reflections.

Months of lockdown took their toll in many ways, but among the most painful was the ban on touching, holding and hugging loved ones. Jesus' words to Mary Magdalene at sunrise on Easter Day have never had such resonance – *Noli me tangere!*, translated variously as 'Do not hold on to me!', 'Do not touch me!' or 'Do not cling to me!' (John 20:17). We can all, now, in some small way, identify with the confusion Mary must have felt when her beloved teacher recoiled from the touch of her hand.

This issue of reflections begins with hands and ends with feet – two moving and intriguing series by Ro Willoughby.

Many of us will be familiar with the prayer of St Teresa of Avila, 'Christ has no body', with its lines: 'Christ has no body but yours, no hands, no feet on earth but yours… Yours are the feet with which he walks to do good, yours are the hands with which he blesses all the world.'

It was so hard when we couldn't be Christ's hands and feet in the world, but Martyn Payne wrote another prayer, for those difficult days: 'God of compassion, who can enter where we cannot go and who can touch those we aren't allowed to hold… Please be our hands and feet, our smile and words, to lighten up their darkness, for nothing is impossible with you.'

God bless you

Eley x

Using these reflections

Perhaps you have always had a special daily time for reading the Bible and praying. But now, as you grow older, you are finding it more difficult to keep to a regular pattern or find it hard to concentrate. Or maybe you've never done this before. Whatever your situation, these Bible reflections aim to help you take a few moments to read God's word and pray, whenever you have time or feel that would be helpful.

When to read them

You may find it helpful to use these Bible reflections in the morning or last thing at night, or any time during the day. There are 40 daily reflections here, grouped around four themes. Each one includes some verses from the Bible, a reflection to help you in your own thinking about God, and a prayer suggestion. The reflections aren't dated, so it doesn't matter if you don't want to read every day. The Bible verses are printed, but if you'd like to read from your own Bible that's fine too.

How to read them

- **Take time** to quieten yourself, becoming aware of God's presence, asking him to speak to you through the Bible and the reflection.
- **Read** the Bible verses and the reflection:
  - What do you especially like or find helpful in these verses?
  - What might God be saying to you through this reading?
  - Is there something to pray about or thank God for?
- **Pray**. Each reflection includes a prayer suggestion. You might like to pray for yourself or take the opportunity to think about and pray for others.

Handed down to us

Ro Willoughby

We use the word 'hand' to mean many things – lending a hand, the height of a horse, a ship's crew member, a round of applause, having something close by. But the most obvious meaning of 'hand' is what moves at the end of our arms.

In this series we look at some of the hands that appear in the Bible, 'handed down' over the centuries. The 'hand' of the Lord is seen in creation and in judgement, in protection and in deliverance. The hands of Jesus are evident throughout the gospels. How do we use our hands?

Being left-handed, I've always been aware of people's hands, on the lookout for other 'cack-handers'. (I was tempted to include Ehud, the Bible's only named left-hander, but decided against him.) As I've been writing, I've been reminded just how much I use my hands not only in daily living but also in my relationships with people, through the sense of touch. I have been reminded how important they are in how I communicate, not just for writing or typing but also in gesticulation and movement, in how I worship and in how I relate to God.

I've made suggestions for what you might do with your own hands in response to what God is saying to you, but let your imagination and memories create other ways of using them.

Above all, hold fast to God, for he is firmly holding you in his hands.

Psalm 95:3–6a (NIV)

Handmade

For the Lord is the great God, the great King above all gods. In his hand are the depths of the earth, and the mountain peaks belong to him. The sea is his, for he made it, and his hands formed the dry land. Come let us bow down in worship.

Where were you when men first landed on the moon in 1969? The recent 50th anniversary celebrations brought back many memories of this extraordinary achievement. Space science has amazingly expanded our knowledge of the universe. Yet so much remains a profound mystery. There are differing theories about just how the world was made, but Jewish and Christian traditions agree it was God who made it, and it belongs to him.

In Genesis, God simply spoke and the created world came into being. God saw that it was good. God does not literally have hands, eyes or a voice box, but the psalmist helps us to picture God's activity as he shaped and moulded this beautiful and efficient world. What's more, God continues to hold 'the whole wide world in his hands', as the familiar song puts it, sustaining and providing for it.

■ PRAYER

Psalm 95 calls us to worship in response. If you can, examine a flower, a leaf or a baby's photo, gazing at it in wonder. Or just look at the intricacy of your own hand. May that inspire you to be grateful to God.

Isaiah 49:15–16a (NIV)

Hand tattoos

'Can a mother forget the baby at her breast and have no compassion on the child she has borne? Though she may forget, I will not forget you! See, I have engraved you on the palms of my hands.'

David Beckham, the English footballer, has at least 40 tattoos on his body, mainly paying tribute to his wife and children, a demonstration of his love for them. Tattooing is currently very popular. I am told that tattoos on the hand attract most attention. They are for people intending to make a very bold statement.

God's people had been forced to live in Babylon for years, far away from their homeland and their city of Jerusalem. They feared that God had left them. How could they worship him in a foreign land? These Bible verses give us two images of God's love for his people. A mother does not confuse her newborn baby with any other baby, even though they've only just got acquainted. This child belongs to her. God loves his people in the same way.

What's more, God cannot forget his people. It is as though our name is tattooed on to the palm of his hand. We may feel insignificant and forgotten by others, but with God that will never happen.

■ **PRAYER**

Hold out your hands, palms up. Imagine your name printed on God's hands. Thank him that he'll never forget you, then pray for anyone you know who feels they no longer matter to anyone.

Psalm 31:14–15 (NIV)

In safe hands

But I trust in you, Lord; I say, 'You are my God.' My times are in your hands; deliver me from the hands of my enemies, from those who pursue me.

There's a vacancy. A new chief executive is needed. Does the organisation appoint someone innovative and prepared to take risks, or a safe pair of hands? The latter sounds reliable and steady but a bit dull, whereas innovation and risk are unpredictable, more progressive... but in the long run, may be more successful.

There are two sorts of hands in these verses. The 'hands of my enemies' belong to those who intend to do harm. The psalmist cries out to God to save and protect him. God's hands will indeed do that. His hands are stronger than those of any enemy.

Our times are also in God's hands. He knows our past, present and future, and he also knows our circumstances. Nothing in our lives can take him by surprise. Look back on your life and remember when God has been with you, both in the good and bad times.

There is nothing dull or risky about God's safe hands. That's why Jesus on the cross could cry out to his Father God, 'Into your hands I commit my Spirit.'

■ PRAYER

I sometimes say to people in need, 'Hold fast to God, because he's holding fast on to you.' Is there something which makes you feel uncomfortable and fearful? Just imagine God holding you firmly in his grip.

Jeremiah 18:3–6 (NIV)

Hand pottery

So I went down to the potter's house, and I saw him working at the wheel. But the pot he was shaping from the clay was marred in his hands; so the potter formed it into another pot, shaping it as seemed best to him. Then the word of the Lord came to me. He said, 'Can I not do with you, Israel, as this potter does?' declares the Lord. 'Like clay in the hand of the potter, so are you in my hand, Israel.'

How often have you seen a potter at the wheel, shaping clay into a round pot? Sometimes it's not quite right, and the clay is lumped together for another attempt. God instructed Jeremiah to watch a potter's hands so that he could understand a simple message. God's people were like clay, to be shaped into objects that were beautiful, regular and useful. God was reminding his people he would judge them for their wrongdoing.

It's a powerful image of God. We rest in his hands as clay. He has shaped us into the people he wants us to be – beautiful, regular and useful. We can reject what he has made us to be, or we can accept and rejoice in it.

■ **PRAYER**

Take a bowl or round plate and let it rest in your hands. Turn it round as you examine it. Imagine yourself resting in the hands of God, the potter, and reflect with thankfulness on how he is still shaping you. 'Have thine own way, Lord! Thou art the Potter, I am the clay. Mould me and make me after thy will.' Amen*

* Adelaide Addison Pollard (1906)

Psalm 47:1; Isaiah 55:12 (NIV, abridged)

Clapping hands

Clap your hands, all you nations; shout to God with cries of joy… You will go out in joy… the mountains and hills will burst into song before you, and all the trees of the field will clap their hands.

I love a concert when the audience is so enthusiastically appreciative that they keep on clapping until the conductor returns to give an encore. Such clapping becomes infectious as we applaud together.

Our gratitude and appreciation of God are evident when we clap in worship or sing loud songs of praise, usually when worshipping with others. This image of trees clapping their hands takes some imagining. Vigorously moving branches would seem odd and dangerous. But the psalmist is using such extravagant language to describe the kind of praise we, along with all of creation, can offer to God.

There is also the clapping of a small child, unable to express happiness in words but doing so with waving arms and uncoordinated taps. We too can 'clap' in our hearts, grateful for God's compassion and commitment to us and his world. We might call this silent clapping, and it is just as real as the exuberant kind. What's more, we offer our thanks to God by the way we live.

■ **PRAYER**

Almighty God, give us such an awareness of your mercies that, with truly thankful hearts, we may show forth your praise, not only with our lips – and our hands – but in our lives, by giving ourselves up to your service. Amen

Psalm 24:3–4a; James 4:8a (NIV)

Clean hands

Who may ascend the mountain of the Lord? Who may stand in his holy place? The one who has clean hands and a pure heart... Come near to God and he will come near to you. Wash your hands, you sinners, and purify your hearts.

It was the Christingle service. I was helping children make their Christingles from an orange. My hands were sticky when I was introduced to the visiting preacher. 'I can't shake hands,' I immediately said. 'I must go and wash them.' You've probably been in similarly embarrassing situations. Have you ever felt unclean when you've come close to God?

Pilgrims climbed up the hill as they came towards the city of Jerusalem. This made the psalmist reflect on how they could prepare themselves to worship God. The answer was to come with clean hands, with hands that had been used to bring glory to God. Our hands help and hinder, create and destroy, welcome and exclude. We can ask God to help us use our hands in ways that please him.

James reminds us that as we come into God's presence, we need to come with spiritually clean hands and a heart that has acknowledged our wrongdoing. We can ask for and receive God's forgiveness.

■ PRAYER

The Lord's Prayer calls us to recognise God our Father, acknowledging our need for forgiveness and deliverance. Then we can come to God in confidence, with clean hands and a pure heart. Why not say that prayer now?

John 13:4–5 (NIV)

Hand-washed

So [Jesus] got up from the meal, took off his outer clothing, and wrapped a towel round his waist. After that, he poured water into a basin and began to wash his disciples' feet, drying them with the towel that was wrapped round him.

When I lead Easter workshops in primary schools, I sometimes ask children to wash one another's feet. Initially this is greeted with groans of disgust, but after talking about it, most children are keen to have a go. Washing dirty, smelly feet isn't particularly pleasant, although feet massaged in warm, soft water is very satisfying.

When Jesus washed his disciples' feet, he wanted them to discover important things about who he was. He had come to serve and set them an example. For some reason, there was no one to wash the disciples' dirty feet before they ate the Passover meal. In a hot, dusty climate, this was normally a servant's job. Jesus took on the task of a servant.

Jesus was showing his commitment to each of them by using his hands to wash their feet. Washing feet is very personal. What's more, by belonging to him, it was as though they had already been made clean. He did not need to wash them all over, just their feet.

■ **PRAYER**

If possible, wash someone's hands or feet or ask someone to do that for you. As you do so, thank Jesus for what he did for his disciples and for each one of us.

Mark 10:14b, 16 (NIV)

Hands that bless

Jesus said to them, 'Let the little children come to me, and do not hinder them, for the kingdom of God belongs to such as these...' And he took the children in his arms, placed his hands on them and blessed them.

Hands are very much in evidence in this story. The disciples probably used their hands to stop parents from bringing their children to Jesus. Jesus would then have used his outstretched hands to welcome the children. This is such a delightful picture – smiling and grateful parents; rebuked, maybe grumpy disciples; and children possibly running into Jesus' arms. Jesus then places his hands upon the children in blessing, allowing God's peace to rest upon them. A never-to-be-forgotten moment.

Of course, God continues to bless us. Sometimes we're conscious of his blessing; often we're not even aware of it. Sometimes his blessing falls on a community or group; sometimes it comes upon an individual. Often a blessing will conclude a service of worship, reminding us of God's desire for us to experience him in all his fulness, all the time.

■ PRAYER

Moses was given these words of blessing for God's people. Say them aloud as God blesses you today. You could also ask God to bless someone else, even though you may not lay hands upon them. 'The Lord bless you and keep you; the Lord make his face shine on you and be gracious to you; the Lord turn his face towards you and give you peace.' Amen*

* NUMBERS 6:24–26

Mark 5:23, 40b–41 (NIV)

Taken by the hand

[Jairus] pleaded earnestly with [Jesus], 'My little daughter is dying. Please come and put your hands on her so that she will be healed and live'... [Jesus] took the child's father and mother and the disciples who were with him, and went in where the child was. He took her by the hand and said to her, '*Talitha koum*!' (which means 'Little girl, I say to you, get up!').

At one stage in our lives, my husband walked our small daughter to school every morning, her little hand wrapped up in his enormous one. This was his daughter, and he was keeping her safe. Precious moments.

Jairus had heard what Jesus could do when it came to healing. If only he could persuade Jesus to lay his hands upon his daughter, all would be well. But she had died before they got home. Jesus simply took her hand and spoke to her. She sat up. He then asked her parents to give her something to eat.

In Mark's gospel Jesus often touched people – he took Simon's mother-in-law by the hand, he put his fingers in the ears of a deaf man, he rubbed his spit on a blind man's eyes to restore his sight. But sometimes he simply spoke in the presence of the sick person or even when he wasn't physically with them. Different situations called for different responses. On this occasion, it was so obviously the right thing for him to take the hand of this little girl.

■ **PRAYER**

If Jesus were to take your hand today, what would you ask him to do?

John 20:19–20 (NIV)

Handprints

[That evening], when the disciples were together, with the doors locked for fear of the Jewish leaders, Jesus came and stood among them and said, 'Peace be with you!' After he said this, he showed them his hands and side. The disciples were overjoyed when they saw the Lord.

I'm sure you know that the fingerprints on every finger of your hand are different, and each hand has different prints. Our fingerprints and the marks on our palms are all unique to us.

On that first Easter evening, Jesus invited his disciples to inspect his hands. They would have immediately recognised him by his carpenter's hands, probably scarred from splinters and accidents and calloused from his tools. They'd have observed his hands over the previous three years as he'd told stories to crowds, eaten meals with them, prayed for and comforted them.

What's more, with the memory of his death still horrifyingly fresh, these hands displayed the scars of nails hammered through them. Yet these weren't the hands of a man who'd just died in excruciating pain, for Jesus was no longer in pain. His resurrection body was more real and alive than any human body. By identifying Jesus' hands, his disciples knew he really was alive. A week later, Thomas was invited to put his hand into the nail prints. Seeing these scars was enough for Thomas to believe.

■ **PRAYER**

Thomas simply said, 'My Lord and my God.' Thank Jesus that he is alive and that death is not the end. We too will have a resurrection body like his.

Signs of glory

John Rackley

If you were asked, 'What are the most significant moments in your life?', what would you choose? Of course, you would choose the ones that mean the most to you.

John makes such a selection from the life of Jesus, then explores what they mean. He believes that each of them reveals the glory of God.

He calls them 'signs'; they point beyond themselves. They reveal how God was at work in the life of Jesus, and each of these moments shines with the presence of God. I pray that this series will help us meet Jesus in a fresh way. At the close of his gospel, John explains clearly why he has written his gospel:

> Now Jesus did many other signs in the presence of his disciples, which are not written in this book. But these are written so that you may come to believe that Jesus is the Messiah, the Son of God and that through believing you may have life in his name.
>
> JOHN 20:30–31 (NRSV)

John 2:6–7 (NRSV)

New from the old

Now standing there were six stone water-jars for the Jewish rites of purification, each holding twenty or thirty gallons. Jesus said to them, 'Fill the jars with water.' And they filled them up to the brim.

When Jesus changes water into wine at a wedding John calls it the first sign.

I expect that you, like me, have things in your home that you hardly ever notice but wouldn't be without. They are just in their usual place – like the six stone water jars in this incident. Jesus used these ordinary things to make something wonderful happen.

The jars are in the background until Jesus made all the difference. John tells us that they were part of the ritual of the Jewish way of life; they were part of an old tradition that had sustained the faith of the Jews for generations. Jesus uses them to do something new and thrilling.

Some people feared that Jesus was going to discard the old way of doing things. He did not. He used the jars to bring joy and laughter to a family celebration. He gave them a fresh purpose. He had come to make the old ways come alive, like the best of wines. It is a sign of God's creative power.

■ **PRAYER**

God of the ages, help me rejoice in your grace and truth, wherever I see them, and accept what is familiar with gratitude and generosity. Amen

John 4:50–53 (NRSV, abridged)

Coincidences happen

Jesus said to him, 'Go; your son will live.' The man believed the word that Jesus spoke to him and started on his way… His slaves met him and told him that his child was alive. So he asked them the hour when he began to recover, and they said to him, 'Yesterday at one in the afternoon the fever left him.' The father realised that this was the hour when Jesus had said to him, 'Your son will live.' So he himself believed, along with his whole household.

I think this father, a royal official, was finding it hard not to be in control. He had a position of influence, but it wasn't helping his son. He wanted his boy to get better. Jesus responded to the deep love of this parent. So when he gets home the father finds the boy and he checks the timing of events. He discovers that the very moment he was sharing his distress with Jesus, his son was getting better, even though he was many miles away. Was it just a coincidence?

We don't always notice coincidences, because we either don't expect them or assume they don't happen. But if we pause and take time to notice, we will see them. Some people call them 'Godincidences'. They suggest that there is more going on than meets the eye.

This is why John selected this incident as the second sign. He is reassuring us that even when matters feel out of control, there is a divine purpose working through everything, and, occasionally, we will notice this.

■ **PRAYER**

God of surprises, help me to take time to see you at work and trust you in times when things feel out of control. Amen

John 6:11, 14 (NRSV)

Incomplete trust

Then Jesus took the loaves, and when he had given thanks, he distributed them to those who were seated; so also the fish, as much as they wanted... When the people saw the sign that he had done, they began to say, 'This is indeed the prophet who is to come into the world.'

Each gospel records an account of a wonderful meal for thousands of people provided by Jesus. It must have been an extraordinary experience. John tells us that people started wondering whether he was a special messenger from God.

It is a moment of exhilaration; they are on the right track. But then things start to go wrong. Some thought this meant Jesus could become king, but Jesus disagrees. He is not fooled by their dreams; he cannot fulfil them.

The people's faith in Jesus starts well, but then they let their own ideas take over.

Any faith in Jesus must not try to be in control. Jesus would not be the servant of false hopes. The people had misread this sign. God's glory was seen in what he provided for them – he was ready to meet their needs but not do just what they wanted. They had to have a patient faith. God knows what we really need.

■ **PRAYER**

God of hope, help me to have a faith based on your teaching and not my fantasies. Amen

John 7:10–12 (NRSV)

Unseen presence

After his brothers had gone to the festival, then [Jesus] also went, not publicly but as it were in secret. The Jews were looking for him at the festival and saying, 'Where is he?' And there was considerable complaining about him among the crowds. While some were saying, 'He is a good man,' others were saying, 'No, he is deceiving the crowd.'

Jesus was a divisive figure. The people of Jerusalem were not sure what to think about him. He created a fascination that also challenged them: was he a good man or did he set out to deceive people?

Jesus was walking among them as they said this, but they did not realise he was there. He was an unseen presence but was aware of what they were saying and would respond later.

We need to be ready for times when our faith in Jesus raises disconcerting questions. It may feel that God is unaware of our questions, or we may think that we can hide them from God. But God is present both when trust in him is easy and when it is hard. He does not always make his presence felt, but that doesn't mean he is absent.

God may not need to do anything obvious for him to be with us, but he always accompanies us through the times when we become confused by him. He is a listening God.

■ **PRAYER**

Listening God, thank you for being with me, even when I am troubled by you. Amen

John 9:24–25 (NRSV)

Clearly convinced

So for a second time they called the man who had been blind, and they said to him, 'Give glory to God! We know that this man is a sinner.' He answered, 'I do not know whether he is a sinner. One thing I do know, that though I was blind, now I see.'

Jesus has healed a blind man on the sabbath. Some people objected to healing on that special day – they thought it made Jesus a sinner – so they questioned the man who was healed.

He gave a clear answer: Jesus had made all the difference to his life. He was not going to be forced to say what they wanted, and so he became a witness to the transforming power of Jesus.

Isn't it wonderful to see someone holding on to their convictions even when people who thought they knew better were challenging him? He is not put off by their questioning. He stands up for what he feels compelled to say. The work of Jesus has given him courage and humility.

He shows courage, because he is not going to be subdued by their status. He has humility, because his sight has been returned by a power greater than him or his questioners. He believes that all of them must give thanks for this sign of God's presence.

■ **PRAYER**

God of comfort, help me to be secure in what I believe. Strengthen anyone who is being challenged for their trust in Jesus. Amen

John 11:41b–44 (NRSV)

Life-giving freedom

Jesus looked upward and said, 'Father, I thank you for having heard me. I knew that you always hear me, but I have said this for the sake of the crowd standing here, so that they may believe that you sent me.' When he had said this, he cried with a loud voice, 'Lazarus, come out!' The dead man came out, his hands and feet bound with strips of cloth, and his face wrapped in a cloth. Jesus said to them, 'Unbind him, and let him go.'

This is the climax of one of the most dramatic gospel stories. John places it at the heart of his gospel. Jesus arrives among grieving people to replace death with life, and calls Lazarus out of his grave. Then he commands him to be released from the cloth that is wound tightly round him. Lazarus walks from the tomb, but needs to be released from his grave clothes; they are no longer needed. Jesus gives Lazarus another chapter in his life.

Jesus is the liberator. Lazarus is released.

Jesus releases us from whatever holds us back from a full life. No barrier, human or otherwise, can withstand the authority of his life-embracing love. When God is at work, we can be released from all that shrouds and constrains our life.

Whenever you feel your limitations, why not read this story and seek the freedom of Spirit, which is God's desire for us?

■ **PRAYER**

God of life, release me from what holds me back from enjoying the embrace – and the freedom – of your love. Amen

John 12:2–3a (NRSV)

Beautiful grace

There they gave a dinner for him. Martha served, and Lazarus was one of those at the table with him. Mary took a pound of costly perfume made of pure nard, anointed Jesus's feet, and wiped them with her hair.

This is a simple act of human kindness. Without a word, Mary does what Jesus needed. She touches him. It is an act of comfort and solace.

Jesus' feet were those of a walker. He had travelled across an often harsh and demanding landscape with few roads, and he had walked the ancient pathways for many months while his destiny was approaching. He knew this, and so did she.

There is no sense of embarrassment on either part. Hers is the touch of love, indifferent to complaints about what was the right thing to do.

She has no interest in joining the debate that Jesus provokes. She is the friend who does what others will not do and is not concerned what they will think. She simply wants Jesus to know that there is someone in his company who understands, and he, in turn, accepts what she is doing.

Together they share a moment of beautiful grace – a sign of divine glory.

■ **PRAYER**

God of graciousness, thank you for friends who have seen my need and put themselves out to help me. Amen

John 12:24 (NRSV)

The way it all works

[Jesus said,] 'Very truly, I tell you, unless a grain of wheat falls into the earth and dies, it remains just a single grain; but if it dies it bears much fruit.'

This brief parable is easily overlooked, but it goes to the heart of the gospel: in God's hands, living and dying are all one.

This simple description of what happens when a grain of wheat is sown may sound primitive to modern minds. A seed falls into the ground and is buried, but it is not the end. It sinks into the earth, but what seems to be at an end is the start of new life.

One seed produces many more. There is an explosion of new life resulting in a wonderful fruitfulness. We see this happening every springtime, and Jesus invites us to appreciate what God is showing us.

The path to fruitfulness may be dark and forbidding. The closing of one life sets up the start of the next. Death is real, but it is not the end of life. Our Saviour assures us that all the goodness in our lives is not wasted and will result in fresh growth.

■ **PRAYER**

God of all life, help me to believe that my life will be fruitful, even when I feel I do not have much to offer others. Amen

John 19:30 (NRSV)

Letting go graciously

When Jesus had received the wine, he said, 'It is finished.' Then he bowed his head and gave up his spirit.

Jesus is dying. The arguments and anger are over, and he has been left by his accusers to face his final moments. His mother and close friends are nearby. He speaks tenderly to them, uniting them in one last act of love.

Now he is alone and approaching his end.

There is no regret. He is ready to depart. The work that he and the Father began is being completed by his death, so there is nothing more to say or do but rest in his Father's embrace. One more sip of wine and he lets go. He bows his head as if in worship and lets his spirit return to his creator.

John invites us to gaze on the serenity of Jesus in his last moments and receive the comfort of God.

We cannot know how we will die, but we can believe that that our life has served a purpose beyond our understanding and rest in the love of God.

■ **PRAYER**

A prayer for the ending of each day: 'Father, into your hands I commit my spirit.' Amen

John 1:14 (NRSV)

The end from the beginning

And the Word became flesh and lived among us, and we have seen his glory, the glory as of a father's only son, full of grace and truth.

For the last 'moment' in this series, we return to the start of John's gospel, which begins with a wonderful poem. It describes what was really going on in the life of Jesus, and it is quite extraordinary.

Jesus is the purpose and meaning of the whole of creation and is walking among people on earth. He offers hope, joy and fulfilment. He lived graciously, with no deceit or cruelty.

We may become anxious about everything which darkens our lives and the lives of other people. But we are in the midst of a creation that abides in the love of God.

We are not drifting helpless in a bleak universe. At its centre is a divine life which pushes back darkness and anxiety. Sometimes all we need is a story of Jesus – a sign of glory – to remind us of this and to restore our faith and our hope in him.

■ PRAYER

Before you pray, look back over this series and ask which reading speaks most powerfully about you and God. Offer him your own prayer of thanksgiving.

The Gift of Years

Debbie Thrower is the pioneer of BRF's Anna Chaplaincy for Older People ministry, offering spiritual care to older people, and is widely involved in training and advocacy.

Visit **annachaplaincy.org.uk** to find out more.

Debbie writes...

One of my favourite photographs of my daughter was taken when she was a child – about two years old – sitting on her grandfather's lap, his gnarled old hands holding her tiny fingers.

I'm glad to see that some of the themes of this issue of Bible reflections deal with our hands and our feet. I'm reminded of the song the late American singer Bill Withers once wrote about his grandmother's hands. He recalled how these were the hands which clapped in church on a Sunday morning, hands which played a tambourine so well. His grandma's hands held many associations for him connected with his childhood.

The fact that Jesus lived an earthly childhood, that he was both fully human and fully divine, lends nobility to our own 'bodiliness'. It helps us to relate to our Saviour in the most basic of ways.

I hope the ideas explored in this edition will help you feel comfortable in your own skin and full of hope for our spiritual bodies when this life is done.

Best wishes

Debbie

Meet Carl Knightly, CEO of Faith in Later Life

Carl Knightly may only be 'halfway to 80', but you would struggle to find a more passionate advocate for the rights and well-being of older people. Now CEO of the recently independent charity Faith in Later Life (**faithinlaterlife.org**), Carl was a career civil servant before moving to the Pilgrims' Friend Society in 2017. Faith in Later Life was created by the Society, and four other Christian charities, to support and resource the faith of older people. After a few months, Carl was invited to lead the work. He is married to Suzy, an intensive care nurse, and they have two young children. Carl has always been active in his local church and currently leads evangelism and outreach ministries, as well as being a governor at his son's school. 'So,' he says, with magnificent understatement, 'there's always lots going on.' We asked him:

What drew you particularly to the role with Faith in Later Life?

I know it sounds like the super-spiritual answer, but I have to say that this is where the Lord has brought me. I never had older people particularly on my heart, until I came to Pilgrims' Friend Society. Don't get me wrong, I love older people; I've always had reverence for older Christians, for my grandparents and so on, but I'd always been involved in issues like poverty, urban ministries, men's ministry, those sorts of things. But you could say that God's got a sense of humour, so I ended up with Pilgrims' Friend Society, with a focus on older people, although mainly because my professional skillset matched the organisation's needs at the time.

But I soon realised that it was a privilege and a blessing to be working among older Christians, and I quickly learned how precious they are, not just in what we can learn from them but because of their example in following the Lord for many years. So when the opportunity was given to me to lead Faith in Later Life, and to spend my time championing older Christians and seeking to reach older people everywhere, I was struck by what a privilege that was, and still is.

Given the range of work that could be done, how would you sum up the main vision of Faith in Later Life?

We want to see older people reached with the good news of Jesus, and see older Christians fulfilled and flourishing. We like Psalm 92:12, 14–15a (NIV):

> The righteous will flourish like a palm tree…
> They will still bear fruit in old age,
> they will stay fresh and green,
> proclaiming, 'The Lord is upright.'

And so we're on a mission to encourage and equip churches to do three things: to reach, serve and empower older people. We want churches to reach out to older people in the wider community, of any faith or none, who may be lonely or may not, and share with them the love of Christ. Mission is right at the heart of what we want to encourage churches to do. It's only when older people, as with any group, come to know the Lord that they know that deep sense of fulfilment. And of equal importance is seeing churches effectively serving and empowering their older Christians.

What is distinctive about the contribution of Faith in Later Life?

It's become evident that there has been a need for this work, and we are quickly becoming a recognised Christian voice for older people. I think that's because we straddle all the different elements in matters to do with later life. There are some Christian organisations that focus more on dementia, say, or retirement, or care homes. We don't want to own anything or compete with anyone, but we're creating a space: we want to be a place where people can come – older people, all people – and work collaboratively, as we seek to shine a spotlight on older Christians and reaching older people in wider society.

Ministries to older people are everyone's business. When speaking about the work of Faith in Later Life, I often ask people if they know any older people. If they fib and say they don't, I ask them if they're hoping to get old one day themselves – as of course everyone is hoping to get old. So this is everyone's business, and it should be everyone's priority. I'm passionate about kids and family ministries, having two young children, but it's not an either/or; as a church, we need to be fully focused on all demographics.

We really want to build community. We are a resource hub, as well as other things, but above all we see ourselves as a movement. We'll see how that plays out over coming years – for now, it's clear there's a need, there's much to do and we would value everyone's prayers.

faithinlaterlife.org

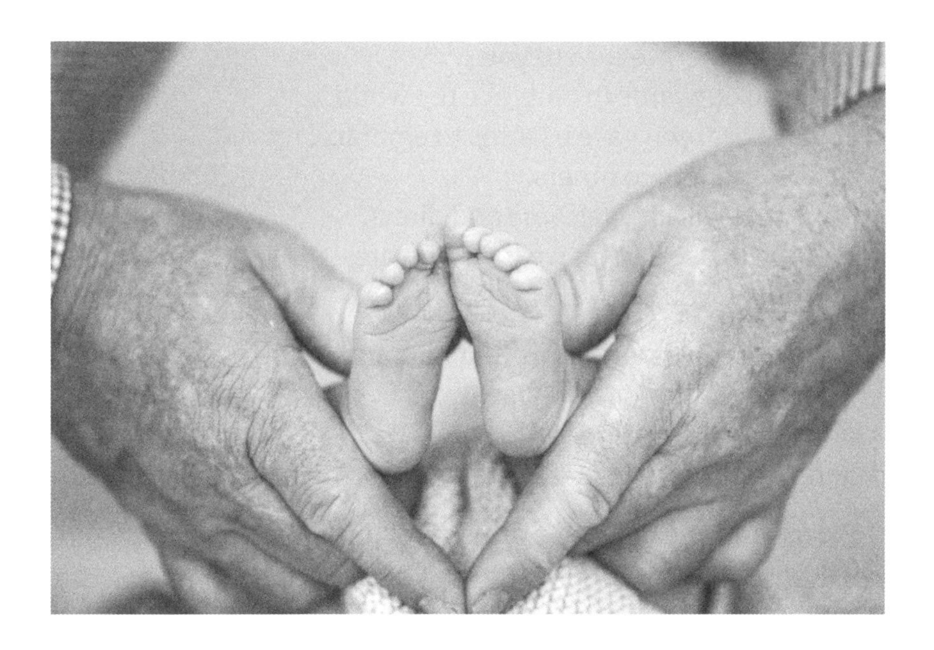

Holy Habits – hands and feet

This prayer is taken from **Holy Habits**, BRF's intergenerational discipleship resources. It perfectly complements Ro Willoughby's reflections on hands and feet.

Gentle Lord, you gave us hands,
that we might hold another.
Hands that can shake, grasp and carry.
May our touch be always tender and loving.
We remember those who face real cruelty at the hands
of others,
and try to understand their fears.
We are reminded that our names are printed on the palms of
your hands,
a fact that we need to highlight and share, in love.

Lord, together we turn to you
and turn outwards to embrace the world.
Loving Lord, you gave us arms to embrace,
to give strength to others.
Arms that will lift, welcome and direct.
We long to use all that we have and are,
to work for you in love.

We are very aware of arms that hurt and abuse,
where love is lacking or absent,
arms that bring sadness,
and we pray for those who suffer the pain of not feeling loved.

We ask that we may have arms of reconciliation and
forgiveness
for those who cause war or conflict.
For those involved in trying to resolve conflict,
we pray that they may have courage, wisdom and humanity.
For those caught up in war and conflict,
we ask for peace, real peace.
Lord, together we turn to you
and turn outwards to embrace the world.

Caring Lord, you gave us feet to walk in your footsteps,
to serve and work for you.
Help us to encourage others to join us on our journey,
encompassing with care and hospitality.
At the same time, we remember those who struggle in life's
journey,
who feel they have lost their way,
as well as those whose feet are no longer fit to make the
physical journey
to be with their congregations.
Use our feet to visit, prayerfully,
lest they feel forgotten.

As refugees in a strange land,
many are walking without direction.
Encourage us as we invite them to join us in fellowship.

Lord, together we turn to you and turn outwards to embrace the world.

From *Holy Habits: Fellowship* (BRF, 2018, p. 17) Search **brfonline.org.uk** for details.

Holy Habits has been pioneered by Andrew Roberts and is based on the ten habits, or practices, described by Luke in his portrait of the early church in Acts 2:42–47. Holy Habits consists of a series of resources – website, booklets, videos and face-to-face training opportunities – designed to encourage the deepening of missional discipleship. Over 200 people of all ages, backgrounds and denominations have contributed to materials for churches, small groups and individuals.

See **holyhabits.org.uk** for more information.

You walk on history – Alan Horner

John Rackley wrote about the signs of God's glory in John's gospel. He reflected on moments in the gospel when a deeper truth broke through and illuminated the everyday with signs of God's presence and power. This poem by the late Alan Horner captures a similar moment in more recent days and shows they still happen, for those with eyes to see.

You walk on history

You walk on history
three feet down
below the pavement
overlaid by years,
and forget it's there.

But now and then
it appears anew
and rears its splendour
for the tourists' eyes:
only so much glory
can we stand.

That goes for their religion too.
The priests and icons,
churches with their domes,
protect the eyes from shining,
but it still breaks through
to pulse like ancient blood
through the astonished heart.

Athens, 1992

From *A Picture With The Paint Still Wet* by Alan Horner. Used with kind permission of his widow, Margaret.

Storms and fair weather

Margot and Martin Hodson

'It looks like rain today.' The British love talking about the weather. Will it rain? Will it stop? Is it a good summer or a hard winter? We all have an opinion. Weather affects people's moods, and they are noticeably more cheerful when it is sunny (but not too hot) and are more irritable when it is wet or cold. Climate change is affecting our weather and causes anxiety, especially to young people.

The Bible is full of weather. Through different weather, God's people learned how to depend on him and how to follow him in all circumstances. The Middle East is very dry, and rain became a metaphor for God's blessing. At times of drought, people prayed for rain, and they also turned to God to work more fully in their lives as they realised how far they had drifted from him.

'It's brightening up a bit' is an optimistic British weather phrase. The rain might be lashing on the windows, but with a slight lightening of the sky we look for sunshine. We hope these reflections guide you to see the brightening hand of God working in your life, through storms and fair weather, to lead you to know him better.

Proverbs 31:21 (NIV)

Well prepared

When it snows, she has no fear for her household; for all of them are clothed in scarlet.

Snow is beautiful, but it is often inconvenient. If you need to get about for whatever reason, it can be hazardous, and many people will fear a serious fall and its consequences. But if you are active and have the right footwear, with a suitable place to take a walk on a sunny, snowy day, it is a magical experience. Looking at a snow scene through a window, while safe in the warmth, can also bring back happy memories of snowball fights and snowmen of old.

Snow is not often expected in Israel, but the woman in Proverbs 31 is very organised. When bad weather comes, she is able to handle it. She runs a big household, is raising a family and even manages a farm, but she is so well prepared that everyone is looked after. Being responsible for other people and managing responsibilities at home and at work can be a real juggling act, and it takes special skill to be prepared when the unexpected happens. But even when those days of responsibility are behind us, building a regular time to pray enables us to be prepared for all weathers and for all that life brings us. Instead of panicking, we can calmly bring our concerns to God and he will show us a way forward.

■ **PRAYER**

Dear Lord, help me to rely on you day by day, so that you prepare me to be calm and trusting, whatever the weather. Amen

Leviticus 26:4 (NIV)

Rain in season

I will send you rain in its season, and the ground will yield its crops and the trees their fruit.

I (Margot) love seasons, and, as each one comes on the horizon, I look forward to the changes in the countryside: the primroses and fresh leaves of spring; summer's colour with long, warm days, or dashing undercover from unexpected rain; crunching through autumn leaves with the glorious golden display on the trees; and even winter, for all its cold and rain, has its special moments when the snow falls and the world stands still.

Now I notice that the seasons are changing. Spring is a little earlier, with bluebells coming out in April rather than May. Golden October is becoming golden November. The summer is more often hotter and drier or much wetter than in years gone by, and the winter is warmer but stormier. In other parts of the world, these changes have led to crop failures when the rains come at the wrong times – or don't come at all – and older people lose their role advising on the best time to plant or harvest.

As our climate changes, it is important to remember that the earth is the Lord's (Psalm 24:1) and that we have a responsibility to care for all he has made. Even small changes, like moving to a renewable energy tariff, not wasting food and other resources, repairing and recycling, will help to secure the seasons' rhythm for future generations.

■ **PRAYER**

Lord, give us courage to change where we need to and to care for your creation entrusted to us. Amen

James 1:6 (NIV)

Tossed by the wind

But when you ask, you must believe and not doubt, because the one who doubts is like a wave of the sea, blown and tossed by the wind.

I (Margot) love sailing but am not an expert. I once got caught in a tidal estuary and was unable to get back to land. However hard my friend and I tried, every small progress was thwarted by the current pushing us back out to sea. We eventually became exhausted and were humble enough to say 'Yes!' when the skipper of a passing motorboat asked us if we needed help. He tossed us a line and towed us into harbour. I clung to that rope for dear life, and I have never felt so relieved to reach dry land.

The apostle James was writing to people who faced difficult situations. They needed wisdom to make decisions and the courage to see them through. Sometimes we know the right decision, but seeing it through can seem like trying to sail a boat against the tide. Prayer is our lifeline, and if we persevere we will find that God will give us strength to face the wind and the waves of difficulties. He will lead us into safe havens.

■ PRAYER

Lord, give us strength to keep going when things get difficult. Give us wisdom to make courageous decisions, when we know they are right. Give us humility to ask for your help when the going gets tough. Amen

Psalm 69:15 (NIV)

Going under

Do not let the floodwaters engulf me or the depths swallow me up or the pit close its mouth over me.

Psalm 69 is attributed to King David, a man who knew many ups and downs in his life. Four verses in the psalm refer to flooding or drowning, suggesting that the writer had some knowledge of this kind of event. Israel is an arid country, but David spent time in the wadis around the Dead Sea while he was hiding as a fugitive from King Saul. For most of the year these are dry, but then rains in the Jerusalem area can rapidly turn the wadis into raging torrents. It is easy for the unwary to be trapped in the wadi, unable to escape as the flood waters rise.

The winter of 2019/20 in the United Kingdom was both the fifth wettest in recorded history and the fifth mildest. The heavy rain caused widespread flooding and considerable damage to property. Homeowners often cleaned up after one flood, only for the waters to return a few weeks later. But we are fortunate in being a rich country with good forecasting and emergency services. Many in poor countries are much less lucky.

■ PRAYER

Pray for those affected by severe weather events, both in the United Kingdom and abroad. Pray too for those trying to bring relief to those affected.

Genesis 9:28 (NIV)

When the storm subsides

After the flood Noah lived 350 years.

Noah's ark is one of the best-known stories in the Bible. Following God's call, Noah builds an ark and saves pairs of every animal and his own family, as a terrible flood wipes out the rest of life. We know Noah the hero, but what happened next?

Noah lived another 350 years, and those years were not without their challenges. A modern reader might wonder if he suffered post-traumatic stress disorder (PTSD) after the trauma of the flood. Might that have led to a sad episode when he became drunk on wine from his vineyard? Or did he simply find it very difficult to settle down to a humdrum life, after such a courageous time? He was fortunate to have sons who came to his aid.

Roles with major responsibility, respect and sometimes fame usually come around the middle of our lives. It can be hard to accept a more ordinary life afterwards, and we can yearn for the days when 'we were somebody'. But when we turn to God, we find that we are infinitely valuable to him, whatever our role or stage in life. He loves us not for *what* we are, but for *who* we are. Moreover, he can guide us in how to spend our gift of years to enrich the lives of others as well as our own.

■ **PRAYER**

Thank you, Lord, for giving me the gift of years. Help me to use these years wisely and joyfully. Amen.

Deuteronomy 8:15 (NIV)

A dry and thirsty land

He led you through the vast and dreadful wilderness, that thirsty and waterless land, with its venomous snakes and scorpions. He brought you water out of hard rock.

After their escape from Egypt, God led the Israelites into the wilderness for 40 years before they entered the promised land. The Sinai Desert is a dry, inhospitable land. There were miracles along the way, like the manna which God sent to feed them, but overall it must have been a difficult time for the people. God tested them and built them into a nation, so that they would be ready for what lay ahead in Israel.

Before Jesus began his public ministry, he was also tested in the wilderness, but this time for 40 days and 40 nights. The number 40 is special in Jewish thought, appearing in many places in the Bible and suggesting the period between two epochs or a very long time period.

Sometimes life can be quite a test, and it can feel as if we are wandering in a wilderness. It may be illness, the loss of a job or bereavement, or we may feel lonely and unwanted. God can seem very distant in these wilderness days, but remembering Jesus' words, 'And surely I am with you always, to the very end of the age' (Matthew 28:20) can really help us get through them.

■ **PRAYER**

Lord Jesus, we pray that you will be with us through all of the trials of life. Amen

Jeremiah 51:16 (NIV)

Stormy weather

When he thunders, the waters in the heavens roar; he makes clouds rise from the ends of the earth. He sends lightning with the rain and brings out the wind from his storehouses.

In February 2020 the Swedish climate activist, Greta Thunberg, came to Bristol to lead a climate strike by the young people of the city and the surrounding area. The city ground to a standstill, and over 25,000 people came, despite the pouring rain.

The 'waters in the heavens' really did roar, and everyone was soaked. Greta, in typical style, told the crowd, 'Our leaders behave like children so it falls to us to be the adults in the room. They are failing us, but we will not back down.'

Like Jeremiah all those years ago, Greta is a prophet. Jeremiah spoke to the people of Israel in Babylon, who were exiled for disobeying God. Greta speaks for her generation against the rich and the powerful. Millions of young people all around the world have joined the climate strike movement as the effects of climate change become ever more obvious. Maybe you know some of the youth and children that have been involved. Maybe you also know some young people who are suffering from anxiety about climate change or having nightmares. Remember them now.

■ **PRAYER**

Lord, we pray for all the young people raising the alarm on climate change and for those who are frightened by it. We also pray for world leaders, that they will take notice. Amen

Matthew 16:2–3 (NIV)

Red sky at night

[Jesus] replied, 'When evening comes, you say, "It will be fair weather, for the sky is red," and in the morning, "Today it will be stormy, for the sky is red and overcast." You know how to interpret the appearance of the sky, but you cannot interpret the signs of the times.'

'Red sky at night, shepherd's delight. Red sky in the morning, shepherd's warning.' It may surprise you to know that this old saying has its origins in the Bible. The Pharisees and Sadducees had come to Jesus, asking him to give them a sign that he was the Messiah. He replied that they knew how to interpret the weather signs, but not the signs of the times. Jesus had already performed many miracles, and it was already clear that he was special.

One of the advantages of age and experience is that we can more easily interpret the signs of our times, or at least we should be able to.

Wisdom can take a long time coming. It can be a very long time before we come to realise that Jesus is the Messiah, the anointed one, and the Son of God. But it is never too late. If you have never before recognised that Jesus is the Messiah, ask him to come into your life. Or maybe you have known Jesus for many years, but long for a family member or friend to come to know him. Pray for them.

■ **PRAYER**

Lord, I pray that you will come into my life and into the lives of my family and friends. Amen

Proverbs 4:18 (NIV)

Bring me sunshine

The path of the righteous is like the morning sun, shining ever brighter till the full light of day.

There are three people whom I (Margot) remember as teenagers, who are now well-known Christian leaders. I remember them as young people with a thriving faith, a passion for ethical principles and vision in their eyes.

It is good to see how their lives have grown and blossomed. They all now carry big responsibilities, have all had to face major challenges and have each made a major difference in the church and wider world. In many ways, they are shining stars among the people I know.

But there are others I remember who have also 'shone brighter' as their lives have progressed. They have not become well known, but they have lived their lives faithfully and well, bringing up families, making thoughtful career choices and becoming backbones of their local churches and communities.

We all have the opportunity to make sunshine in this world. It leads some people to take up major and high-profile roles, but for most people making sunshine is about living our lives well: honestly, faithfully and conscientiously and, when we have made mistakes, being willing to admit them.

When we next see the sunrise, let's ask God to give us a fresh opportunity to share his love and make sunshine.

■ **PRAYER**

Lord, give us a vision for where we might bring light and hope to those around us. Amen

1 Kings 19:11b–12 (NIV)

In a whisper

Then a great and powerful wind tore the mountains apart and shattered the rocks before the Lord, but the Lord was not in the wind. After the wind there was an earthquake, but the Lord was not in the earthquake. After the earthquake came a fire, but the Lord was not in the fire. And after the fire came a gentle whisper.

Elijah is in big trouble. He has defeated and killed the prophets of Baal, but then the evil queen, Jezebel, promises to have him killed by the next day. This throws Elijah into a major depression, and he has had enough and wishes he could die. An angel comes and encourages him to eat, and he then travels 40 days and 40 nights to Mount Horeb.

There, on the mountain, God shows Elijah something important. God says that he will pass by. Then a wind comes up, so strong that it can tear mountains apart. But Elijah does not sense God in the wind. There follows an earthquake, and finally a fire, but God is not in either. Then comes a gentle whisper. God does not speak to Elijah in the wind, the earthquake or the fire, but in a whisper.

And so it can be for us. God frequently speaks to us not by spectacular signs, but in a whisper. He is often there in the quiet as the 'still, small voice of calm'. How can we learn to listen for the voice and for the whisper?

■ **PRAYER**

Lord God, I pray that you will speak clearly to me today, whether in the wind, earthquake or fire, or in a quiet whisper. Amen

Feet made for walking

Ro Willoughby

My three-year-old grandson was seriously tired. He didn't want to walk any further. He's too heavy to carry but, somehow, we had to get home. How many ways of moving forward could I think of? Walking on tiptoe, stamping, marching, running, hopping, striding, leaping off a doorstep, long jumps over a manhole cover, balancing along the bus shelter seat or along the low wall at the corner. His feet are made for walking, and we made it.

Over the decades, our feet have taken us hundreds of thousands of miles, to places we wanted to go to and those we didn't. We've clambered over rocks, danced and trudged. We've had sore feet and flexible feet. Our feet may now be less mobile and more troublesome. We may be very aware of what our feet can no longer do.

Spiritually, we have walked on the journey of faith, accompanied by Christ. That journey also will have made us weary, joyful, heavy-hearted, lost and thankful. Our spiritual feet have played an essential part in following Christ.

In this series, we'll hear about the occasions when Jesus showed concern for the feet of others. We'll look at Jesus' own feet, where they took him and what happened to them. We'll end with a reflection on our own feet. So come with me and let's walk together to the feet of Jesus.

John 5:8–9a (NIV)

Jesus heals lame feet

Then Jesus said to him, 'Get up! Pick up your mat and walk.' At once the man was cured; he picked up his mat and walked.

Jane travels to church in her mobility scooter. Slowly she transfers herself to a front pew. Her feet, once so energetic and flexible, are no longer so. Her family and many friends at church support her. She'd like Jesus to heal her but accepts she may have to wait for heaven. While she waits, her faith in Christ remains strong.

The man in this story hadn't been able to walk for 38 years. Someone must have brought him to the pool of Bethesda in Jerusalem. Unlike Jane, there is no indication that the man had any faith in Jesus or knew anything about him. We are told, though, that he had faith that the first person into the pool after the water was strangely rippled would be healed. He hoped someone would help him be first, but whoever brought him didn't wait with him. All alone, he was doomed to failure.

Jesus' power to heal did not depend on rippling water. He simply had power to heal because he was God and he had compassion on the lame man. This man was to learn that faith in Jesus is what really matters. He obeyed Jesus, and his broken feet were made whole. He walked away.

■ PRAYER

Do you know someone who is waiting, keeping their fingers crossed in the hope that something will happen to transform their sorrow or difficult situation? Pray for them and ask Jesus to make himself known to them. That's what really matters.

John 13:4–5 (NIV)

Jesus washes dirty feet

[Jesus] **got up from the meal, took off his outer clothing and wrapped a towel round his waist. After this he poured water into a basin and began to wash his disciples' feet, drying them with the towel that was wrapped round him.**

As I mentioned in an earlier reflection called 'Hand-washed', around Easter time, I lead workshops in primary schools to explore the Easter story with classes of children. I ask them to think of messy jobs at home that no one likes doing. Their suggestions include changing a baby sister's nappy or cleaning dog poo off a shoe. I then tell them the story of Jesus' last meal with his disciples. The children don't like the idea of foot-washing.

For some reason, when the disciples ascended to the upper room to celebrate the Passover feast, there was no servant to welcome them or wash the dust off their dirty feet. We can imagine them looking around indignantly for the person whose job it was. This was an unpleasant job, suitable only for an insignificant servant.

So we can imagine their shock when Jesus himself washes and tends the feet of each of his disciples. After sitting down, he told them that he had set them an example that they also should serve others, however unpleasant it might be. Washing feet has become a symbol of service, putting the needs of others before our own needs, however unpleasant. If Jesus could do this, then so should we.

■ **PRAYER**

If you can, rest your feet in a bowl of warm, soapy water as you pray: Lord Jesus, help me today to serve someone else, however much I may not want to. Help me to follow the example of Jesus. Amen.

Mark 5:22–23 (NIV)

Pleading at Jesus' feet

Then one of the synagogue leaders, named Jairus, came, and when he saw Jesus, he fell at his feet. He pleaded earnestly with him, 'My little daughter is dying. Please come and put your hands on her so that she will be healed and live.'

Most parents will do almost anything if their child is in need or in danger. We read of parents who implore hospital authorities to carry out a new treatment that could possibly improve their child's condition. They would willingly donate one of their own organs.

Here is one such parent, Jairus, whose twelve-year-old daughter was dying. It is probable that as a leader in the synagogue, he had suspicions of Jesus and his teaching. What's more, he was a respectable member of the community, so falling at Jesus' feet was humiliating. But in coming to Jesus, he had come in desperation to the right person.

Jairus' faith in Jesus was further tested, because their walk to his home was interrupted. It took them longer to arrive, by which time his daughter had died. But for Jesus, this was not a problem. He restored the little girl to life.

■ **PRAYER**

You may no longer be easily able to kneel on the ground, but picture yourself at the feet of Jesus. Urgently tell him about what might be deeply troubling you. Jesus will hear, he will respond, but as with Jairus, there may be a delay.

Luke 7:44–47 (NIV, abridged)

Washing Jesus' feet

[Jesus] said to Simon [the Pharisee], 'Do you see this woman? I came into your house. You did not give me any water for my feet, but she wet my feet with her tears... [She] has not stopped kissing my feet... She has poured perfume on my feet. Therefore, I tell you, her many sins have been forgiven – as her great love has shown.'

Simon the Pharisee had invited Jesus to his home for a meal, along with some religious leaders. They reclined around a low table. On arrival, the custom was to wash the dirty feet of a guest. Simon failed to do this.

The woman in this story had almost certainly met Jesus before. She had a bad reputation and was overwhelmingly grateful to him that he valued her and had forgiven her for her sins. She wanted to show her gratitude. She spotted him entering the house and, since the doors were open for anyone to come inside, she followed Jesus. She didn't care if she made an exhibition of herself in giving Jesus' feet a dramatic foot massage. He was not embarrassed.

Unlike Simon, who judged Jesus, she loved him extravagantly. Deep in her heart, she knew Jesus loved her. More than anything, she wanted him to know that.

■ PRAYER

'Jesus loves me – this I know; for the Bible tells me so; little ones to him belong – they are weak, but he is strong.' Let this old children's song remind you of Jesus' love for you and be grateful.*

* 'Jesus Loves Me', Anna B. Warner (1860)

Luke 10:39–42 (NIV, abridged)

Sitting at Jesus' feet

Martha had a sister called Mary, who sat at the Lord's feet listening to what he said. But Martha was distracted by all the preparations that had to be made. She came to him and asked, 'Lord, don't you care that my sister has left me to do the work by myself? Tell her to help me!' 'Martha, Martha,' the Lord answered, you are worried and upset about many things... Mary has chosen what is better.'

We have just moved into a modern new house, which has a kitchen diner. In our last home, the small kitchen was far away from the dining room. So soon after guests arrived, I would disappear to prepare the meal. Now, when entertaining, we can prepare food and talk with our friends at the same time. It's great.

I imagine that when Jesus arrived at the home of Lazarus, Martha and Mary, he didn't sit down where the food was being prepared. Martha and her sister had a choice – to sit with their much-loved guest or to prepare the meal.

Mary chose to sit at Jesus' feet. The food could wait. But Martha was uncomfortable with that idea. We can imagine her getting more and more fed up with her sister as she prepared the meal without Mary's help. Jesus gently reminded Martha that being with him was the best option. He gently invites us to be with him, simply to enjoy his company and to hear his words.

■ **PRAYER**

May the grace of our Lord Jesus Christ, the love of God and the fellowship of the Holy Spirit be with us all, evermore. Amen

Luke 24:36–39 (NIV, abridged)

Touching Jesus' feet

Jesus himself stood among [the disciples] and said to them, 'Peace be with you.' They were... frightened, thinking they saw a ghost. He said to them, 'Why are you troubled, and why do doubts rise in your minds? Look at my hands and my feet... Touch me and see; a ghost does not have flesh and bones, as you see I have.'

Jesus' disciples had seen Jesus arrested and crucified on the cross, with nails in his hands and nails in his feet. They knew he was truly dead and buried. They feared for their own safety. But two days later some of the women in the group said they'd actually seen Jesus alive. Peter and John had also seen that his tomb was empty. We can imagine their bewilderment and their doubts.

On Easter Day evening, two disciples burst in and announced that they'd just had a conversation with Jesus, alive again, but as soon as they recognised him, he had disappeared. No wonder, then, that the disciples were really frightened when Jesus himself appeared as they ate their meal. As evidence he was no ghost, Jesus invited them to touch the nail marks in his hands and feet. His disciples were convinced: Jesus is alive!

We cannot literally touch Jesus' feet. But his wounded feet remind us of his great suffering. They also assure us that death was not the end. He had a new body. He was no ghost.

■ **PRAYER**

Thank you, Jesus, that because of your great pain on the cross, you understand my suffering. Give me strength and comfort today if I am in pain or bewildered or am weary. Amen

Acts 1:9–11a (NIV)

Disappearing feet

After [Jesus] said this, he was taken up before their very eyes, and a cloud hid him from their sight. They were looking intently up into the sky as he was going, when suddenly two men dressed in white stood beside them. 'Men of Galilee,' they said, 'why do you stand here looking into the sky?'

A group of children and I were making Christmas angels. We were discussing whether angels have wings or not. One boy asked me if Jesus had wings so he could fly to heaven after his resurrection. We decided he didn't. The same boy then said he thought God reached a big hand out of the sky and yanked Jesus upwards.

We don't know how Jesus ascended to heaven 40 days after his resurrection. But we do know he went upwards and his disciples watched him go. It is probable that the last thing they saw of him was his feet.

I'm glad Jesus returned to heaven. His job was done. He had made it possible for all people to receive forgiveness and to be made right with God.

Just occasionally, someone asks me to explain to another person on their behalf, the reason why they may have seemed rude and standoffish the last time they spoke. Jesus is like that for us. In heaven, he is now interceding to God, his Father, on our behalf.

■ **PRAYER**

We may sometimes wonder if God understands us. Because Jesus was a human being just like us, he knows what it is like and so is able to speak with understanding. Tell Jesus about anything that is troubling you. Be certain he understands and is praying for you.

Ephesians 6:13–15 (NIV, abridged)

Strong shoes on my feet

Put on the full armour of God, so that when the day of evil comes, you may be able to stand your ground, and after you have done everything, to stand. Stand firm, then… with your feet fitted with the readiness that comes from the gospel of peace.

Recently I bought some new, light walking shoes. They have made the hill-walking I enjoy even more pleasurable, because the grip on the soles is so effective. I'm far less likely to slip than I was with my old boots. Much can be said for strong shoes, although most people at some point have favoured fashion over comfort.

Roman soldiers at the time of the apostle Paul were equipped with shoes for long marches that had small spikes in the soles for a strong grip. When fighting in battle, they were stable, ready to fight, less likely to be felled to the ground. Paul urged the Christians in Ephesus to put on all the armour of God, so that they would be confident to stand up for what they knew was true about the good news of Jesus.

There may be times when we question God, wondering why there's so much evil in the world. Does God still care for us?

He does. We can be confident that he keeps his word. Through Christ's death, we can have peace with God. He enables us to stand firm, like a soldier ready for battle. God will not fail us.

■ PRAYER

*Use the words of this hymn to talk with God about standing confident and firm in him. 'Soldiers of Christ, arise, and put your armour on, strong in the strength which God supplies, through his eternal Son.'**

* 'Soldiers of Christ, Arise', Charles Wesley (1749)

Psalm 18:33 (NIV)

My feet on a high rock

He makes my feet like the feet of a deer; he causes me to stand on the heights.

A few years ago, while on holiday in Normandy, I spent some time reflecting on one of my favourite psalms, Psalm 18. It's a psalm that is addressed to 'my rock, my fortress and my deliverer'. It's full of images of how God relates to us. For example, 'He reached down from on high and took hold of me' (v. 16).

As we climbed Mont St Michel, the monastery rising high on a rock above the sandy beach at low tide, I felt I was 'standing on the heights' (v. 33). For many centuries, those living in the monastery have been protected from the force of the sea and from the danger of those from the mainland who wished them ill.

The writer of this psalm invites us to think of ourselves with feet of a deer, moving quicker and more nimbly than we could ever do, being taken by God to that high place. Here we are safe, and here we can look down on all around us, maybe to see things from God's perspective.

■ **PRAYER**

Over the years, many songs have been written using these words from Psalm 18, songs of praise and gratitude to God. You may not be able to recall such a song right now, so use the words of the psalm to thank God that over your life he has taken you, with the feet of a deer, to places you would not expect. He continues to keep you safe.

Psalm 18:36; 119:105 (NIV)

My feet on a broad path

You provide a broad path for my feet, so that my ankles do not give way... Your word is a lamp for my feet, a light on my path.

On that same holiday in Normandy, when I was reflecting on one of my favourite psalms, Psalm 18, we were staying in a cottage deep in the forest, criss-crossed by many well-maintained, flat roads and pathways. When we were walking along, we were thankful for these smooth surfaces. There was little to make us stumble (although there was plenty of scope to get lost, especially in the dark).

In the psalms, there are many verses about God guiding his people along the right path (Psalm 25), God keeping our feet from slipping (Psalm 66), God with us when we're walking in the darkest valley so there's no need to be afraid (Psalm 23). Here in Psalm 18, we have God providing a safe, clear path to walk along.

Of course, there are many obstacles along life's pathway. It's sometimes tough, and we may not always be able to see the way ahead. But God continues to walk protectively with us. However, ultimately it is we who walk with him. A well-known hymn includes the words: 'He knows the way he taketh, and I will walk with him.'*

■ PRAYER

Look at your feet and thank God especially for the places where you have walked and have felt especially close to him. May you continue to walk together with God along that broad pathway. 'My steps have held to your paths; my feet have not stumbled' (Psalm 17:5).

* 'In Heavenly Love Abiding', Anna L. Waring (1850)

There is a time for everything...

> **There is a time for everything, and a season for every activity under the heavens: a time to be born and a time to die... a time to kill and a time to heal, a time to tear down and a time to build, a time to weep and a time to laugh.**
> ECCLESIASTES 3:1–4 (NIV, abridged)

I feel intimidated by the task before me: writing something now, in mid-June, that will still be of substance when you read it early next year. Yet, I have good cause for confidence.

While coronavirus has affected us all, some in ways that will never be forgotten, there is comfort in scripture. Ecclesiastes tells us that there is a time for everything – a season comes, and a season goes. Jesus warns us not to store up treasures for ourselves on earth, but rather to place our hope fully in the heavenly kingdom, where good things do not end and where every tear is wiped away.

These truths do not remove the pain we feel now. They do give hope beyond it.

BRF's work is to share timeless truths and an unswerving hope with an ever-changing world – work that requires we adapt to make a difference in every generation. Much of what we do today – and God willing into the future – is funded by donations and gifts in wills.

I'd like to invite you to prayerfully consider whether you could support this work through a gift in your will. If you would like further information about leaving a gift in your will to BRF, please get in touch with us on **+44 (0)1235 462305**, via **giving@brf.org.uk** or visit **brf.org.uk/lastingdifference**.

Martin Gee
Fundraising manager

PS: Please be assured that whatever decision you reach about your will, you don't need to tell us and we won't ask. May God grant you wisdom as you reflect on these things.

TRYSTAN OWAIN HUGHES
OPENING OUR LIVES
Devotional readings for Lent
BRF LENT BOOK

Inspired by Neil MacGregor's Radio 4 programme, 'A History of the World in 100 Objects', Gordon Giles spends each week in a different room gleaning spiritual lessons from everyday household objects. As a result, you might discover that finding God in the normal pattern of life – even in the mundane – transforms how you approach each day. Running as a thread through it all are the seven Rs of Lent: regret, repentance, resolution, recognition, reconciliation, renewal and resurrection.

At Home in Lent
An exploration of Lent through 46 objects
Gordon Giles
978 0 85746 589 4 £8.99
brfonline.org.uk

To order

Online: **brfonline.org.uk**
Telephone: +44 (0)1865 319700
Mon–Fri 9.30–17.00
Post: complete this form and send to the address below

Delivery times within the UK are normally 15 working days. Prices are correct at the time of going to press but may change without prior notice.

Title	Issue*	Price	Qty	Total
Holy Habits: Fellowship		£4.99		
Opening Our Lives		£8.99		
At Home in Lent		£8.99		
Bible Reflections for Older People (single copy)	May/Sep* 21	£5.25		

**delete as appropriate*

POSTAGE AND PACKING CHARGES			
Order value	**UK**	**Europe**	**Rest of world**
Under £7.00	£2.00	Available on request	Available on request
£7.00–£29.99	£3.00		
£30.00 and over	FREE		

Total value of books	
Postage and packing	
Total for this order	

Please complete in BLOCK CAPITALS

Title .... First name/initials .... Surname..

Address ....

.... Postcode ....

Acc. No. .... Telephone ....

Email ....

Method of payment

❑ Cheque (made payable to BRF) ❑ MasterCard / Visa

Card no. ☐☐☐☐ ☐☐☐☐ ☐☐☐☐ ☐☐☐☐

Expires end M M Y Y Security code* ☐☐☐ Last 3 digits on the reverse of the card

Signature* .... Date ..../........./.........

*ESSENTIAL IN ORDER TO PROCESS YOUR ORDER

Please return this form to:
BRF, 15 The Chambers, Vineyard, Abingdon OX14 3FE | enquiries@brf.org.uk
To read our terms and conditions, please visit **brfonline.org.uk/terms**.

BROP0121

BIBLE REFLECTIONS FOR OLDER PEOPLE GROUP SUBSCRIPTION FORM

All our Bible reading notes can be ordered online
by visiting **biblereadingnotes.org.uk/subscriptions**

The group subscription rate for ***Bible Reflections for Older People*** will be £15.75 per person until April 2022.

☐ I would like to take out a group subscription for .... (*quantity*) copies.

☐ Please start my order with the May 2021 / September 2021 / January 2022* issue.
(**delete as appropriate*)

Please do not send any money with your order. Send your order to BRF and we will send you an invoice.

Name and address of the person organising the group subscription:

Title .... First name/initials .... Surname..

Address...

.... Postcode ....

Telephone .... Email ....

Church...

Name and address of the person paying the invoice if the invoice needs to be sent directly to them:

Title .... First name/initials .... Surname..

Address...

.... Postcode ....

Telephone .... Email ....

Please return this form to:

BRF, 15 The Chambers, Vineyard, Abingdon OX14 3FE | enquiries@brf.org.uk
To read our terms and conditions, please visit **brfonline.org.uk/terms**.

BROP0121

BIBLE REFLECTIONS FOR OLDER PEOPLE INDIVIDUAL/GIFT SUBSCRIPTION FORM

To order online, please visit **brfonline.org.uk/collections/subscriptions**

☐ I would like to take out a subscription (*complete your name and address details only once*)
☐ I would like to give a gift subscription (*please provide both names and addresses*)

Title .... First name/initials .... Surname ....

Address ....

.... Postcode ....

Telephone .... Email ....

Gift subscription name ....

Gift subscription address ....

.... Postcode ....

Gift message (*20 words max. or include your own gift card*):

....

....

Please send ***Bible Reflections for Older People*** beginning with the May 2021 / September 2021 / January 2022* issue (**delete as appropriate*):

(*please tick box*)	**UK**	**Europe**	**Rest of world**
Bible Reflections for Older People	☐ £19.95	☐ £27.45	☐ £31.50

Total enclosed £ .... (*cheques should be made payable to 'BRF'*)

Please charge my MasterCard / Visa ☐ Debit card ☐ with £ ....

Card no. ☐☐☐☐ ☐☐☐☐ ☐☐☐☐ ☐☐☐☐

Expires end ☐☐ ☐☐ Security code* ☐☐☐ Last 3 digits on the reverse of the card

Signature* .... Date ....../....../......

*ESSENTIAL IN ORDER TO PROCESS YOUR ORDER

Please return this form to:

BRF, 15 The Chambers, Vineyard, Abingdon OX14 3FE | enquiries@brf.org.uk

To read our terms and conditions, please visit **brfonline.org.uk/terms**.

BROP0121